Tootsie the Tapping Fairy

TOOTSIE
THE TAPPING
FAIRY

Story & Pictures by
Jo Barker

Published in Australia in 2020 by Tap Happy
www.taphappy.com.au

Text and illustrations copyright © Joanne Barker, 2020

This book is copyright. Apart from any fair dealing for the purposes of private study, research, criticism or review permitted under the Copyright Act 1968, no part may be stored or reproduced by any process without prior written permission. Enquiries should be made to the publisher.

National Library of Australia
Cataloguing-in-Publication data:
Author: Barker, Joanne
Tootsie the Tapping Fairy / written and illustrated by Joanne Barker
ISBN 978-0-6487176-0-7

Printed in Australia by IngramSpark

For my beautiful grandchildren:
Ava, Isaac, Zoe, Rafferty and Lucy.
You all hold a very special place in my heart.

On the morning of her 7th birthday, Tootsie sat tapping her feet with excitement as she looked at the beautifully wrapped present she had just received from her Mum and Dad.

She quickly tore off the ribbons and paper and opened the box to find a gorgeous pair of sparkly, pink tap shoes inside.

Tootsie was absolutely thrilled.

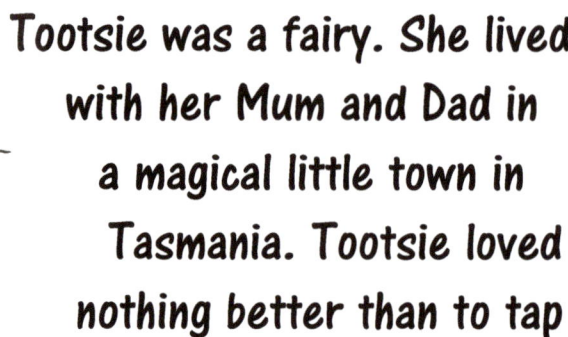

Tootsie was a fairy. She lived with her Mum and Dad in a magical little town in Tasmania. Tootsie loved nothing better than to tap her feet all day long. She tapped inside at home, she tapped when she was outside playing, she tapped at the shops, she tapped her way down the street to meet her friends, and she tapped all the way to school. In fact, she even tapped her feet all day long in the classroom, driving her teacher nuts. She just couldn't keep her feet still. Her new tap shoes were the perfect birthday present.

'We have another surprise for you Tootsie!' said Tootsie's dad, Tiddles. 'We thought you might enjoy having some tap dancing lessons at Miss Twinkle's Sparkly Tapping School. Your first lesson will be after school today.'

'Oh, wow! Thanks Mum, thanks Dad! This has got to be the best birthday present ever!'

Tootsie had a great day at school. Her classmates sang "Happy Birthday" to her in the morning, and she got some free time as a birthday treat in the afternoon. When the bell rang at 3:30

though, Tootsie squealed with delight as she ran out to meet her Mum. It was time for her very first tap dancing lesson.

'Tootsie, you're a natural!'

'Tootsie, that's brilliant!'

'Tootsie, that's fantastic!'

These were just some of the comments Tootsie received from Miss Twinkle as she danced her way through her first lesson. It was just like a beautiful, happy dream.

'Come on Tootsie, hurry up! Nana Flo and Grandpa are coming over for dinner and cake to celebrate your birthday!' called Mum, as soon as Tootsie had finished tapping her way through her last dance.

Even though she would have loved to keep dancing, Tootsie quickly ran into the change room. She pulled her tap shoes off, popped her sneakers on, and threw on her jacket. She grabbed her bag and ran to the door where her Mum was waiting. Tootsie was always very excited to see her grandparents.

When they arrived home, it was time for a delicious birthday dinner followed by a beautiful, big, birthday cake. Tootsie's cake was decorated with – you guessed it – tap shoes!

'Nana Flo and Grandpa, can I show you my real tap shoes now?' asked Tootsie when dinner was finished.

She raced off to her bedroom, without waiting for an answer.

Next thing, there was an almighty howl from Tootsie's bedroom.

'NOOOO, I CAN'T BELIEVE IT! MY SHOES AREN'T IN MY BAG!'

Tootsie howled and wailed and screamed and stomped her feet, and had one of the biggest tantrums she'd ever had. Tootsie was generally pretty happy, but, when things went wrong, boy, did she have a temper!

'Oh dear,' said her mum Myrtle, as she rolled her eyes. 'Here we go again. Tootsie must have left her shoes at the dance studio in all the rush.'

'Leave her to me,' said Nana Flo, 'I'll see what I can do to help.' Off she went into Tootsie's bedroom.

'Now Tootsie, I can see that you're very upset,' said Nana Flo between Tootsie's tears. 'We don't want this to spoil your birthday though, do we? I have an idea. You know how you love to tap?'

'Yes,' replied Tootsie, with tears streaming down her face.

'Well, I know a different sort of tapping that might help you to feel better. Magic tapping. Would you like me to show you?' Tootsie nodded.

She knew Nana Flo, who was also a fairy godmother, had lots of wonderful magic tricks.

'Do you know that there are magical parts on your hands, head and body that you can tap with your fingers?' Tootsie shook her head. 'Doing this will magically tell your brain to feel calm, and can help you to feel much better. What are you mostly feeling right now, Tootsie?'

'(Sniff sniff) ... I'm pretty **ANGRY** with myself for forgetting to bring my tap shoes home. I'm **DISAPPOINTED** that I can't show them to you. But I'm mostly, (sniff sniff) just **SAD** because I haven't got them, and I'll have to wait until we can go back to see Miss Twinkle to get them back!' howled Tootsie.

'Ok. Well how about we start by tapping on being **SAD** then,' said Nana Flo. 'Where do you feel the sadness, Tootsie?'

'(Sniff) ... In my tummy.'

'Alright Tootsie. I'd like you to try to give your sadness a score. If one was the least sadness you could feel, and ten was the very worst, what would your number be?'

'A nine,' replied Tootsie who was still quite teary.

And so they began.

'We start by tapping on the side of our hand, Tootsie. We call this the karate chop point. Whilst we tap on the karate chop point, we talk about how we feel, and what is bothering us.'

Tootsie knew about karate chops, because Nana Flo won a gold medal for karate in the Fairy Olympics last year.

She copied what Nana Flo was doing and saying.

'**EVEN THOUGH I FEEL REALLY SAD IN MY TUMMY BECAUSE I HAVEN'T GOT MY TAP SHOES HERE TONIGHT...**' said Nana Flo.

So Tootsie repeated, '**EVEN THOUGH I FEEL REALLY SAD IN MY TUMMY BECAUSE I HAVEN'T GOT MY TAP SHOES HERE TONIGHT...**'

'**I'M A GREAT KID ANYWAY,**' said Nana Flo.

'**I'M A GREAT KID ANYWAY,**' repeated Tootsie, tapping on the side of her hand.

They said this and tapped on their karate chop points, three times.

Then they tapped together on the top of their heads. Nana Flo said, **'I FEEL SO SAD.'**

Tootsie repeated the same words, tapping on the top of her head at the same time.

Next, they tapped on the start of their eyebrows, **'ALL THIS SADNESS IN MY TUMMY,'** said Nana Flo.

Tootsie repeated, **'ALL THIS SADNESS IN MY TUMMY.'**

The side of their eyes, right on the edge of the bone you can feel there, was the next point. They tapped on that with Tootsie repeating after Nana Flo, **'I REALLY WANTED TO SHOW NANA FLO AND GRANDPA!'**

Then they tapped under their eyes. **'I'M FEELING SO VERY SAD,'** said Nana Flo.

'I'M FEELING SO VERY SAD,' repeated Tootsie.

After that, they tapped under their noses, saying **'I'M SO SAD; I WISH I HAD THEM NOW.'**

The next point was on their chins, on the little crease under their mouths. They said, **'I'M REALLY SAD ABOUT MY TAP SHOES.'** Tootsie had almost stopped crying now.

Just under her collarbone was the next point for Tootsie to tap on. **'I REALLY WANT MY TAP SHOES, BUT THEY'RE NOT HERE, AND I CAN'T GET THEM TONIGHT,'** continued Nana Flo, and Tootsie repeated.

The last place to tap was a little bit below their armpits. Tootsie thought she must have looked like a monkey when she tapped here. '**ALL THIS SADNESS IN MY TUMMY. I'M SO SAD,**' said Nana Flo.

'**ALL THIS SADNESS IN MY TUMMY. I'M SO SAD,**' said Tootsie.

After they had tapped through all of those magic points, Nana Flo asked Tootsie to give a score out of ten for how she was feeling now.

'I actually feel a bit better!' replied Tootsie, who was really quite surprised. 'I think my sad feeling is a three now, but it's still in my tummy a bit.'

'What a great improvement, that's wonderful Tootsie! Let's see if we can get that score any lower by doing one more round of magic tapping.'

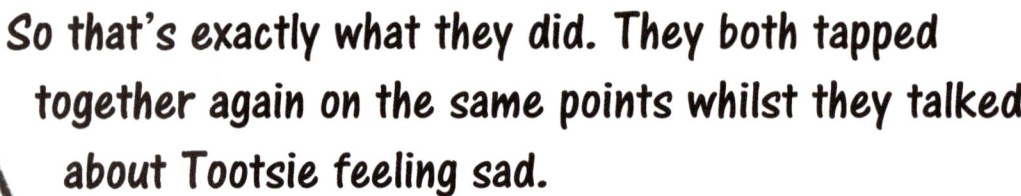

So that's exactly what they did. They both tapped together again on the same points whilst they talked about Tootsie feeling sad.

'Wow, that is great magic!' smiled Tootsie. 'It worked. I don't feel sad at all, and I don't feel angry or disappointed like I did before, either! I know my tap shoes are safe with Miss Twinkle and I'll get them back tomorrow.'

'Excellent,' said Nana Flo with a big smile on her face. 'I'm going to show you one more magic trick Tootsie. Sometimes, when you're sad, angry, frightened or worried, it might be a bit difficult to tap on all of those points. So for times like that, you can just tap on the side of your fingers, right next to your fingernails, and nobody else has to know.'

Nana Flo quickly showed Tootsie, who really just wanted to race back to the kitchen to have another piece of birthday cake, but she got the general idea.

Much to everyone's delight, Tootsie was happy for the rest of the evening, and didn't worry about her tap shoes again. She knew she'd learned some really special magic that night. It was a great birthday!

The next morning, Tootsie arrived at school and was greeted at the front gate by her friends, Ava and Isaac. They said hello but Tootsie could tell that they weren't their usual happy selves.

'What's up?' Tootsie asked.

'Oh, we've got our flying test today,' said Ava. 'Last time I tried to fly, I crashed, BANG, straight into the garden!'

'Yeah, and I couldn't even get off the ground,' added Isaac. 'I'm really worried.'

'Me too,' said Ava

'Mmmmmm,' thought Tootsie, remembering what she and Nana Flo had done last night. 'I might be able to help here.'

She told her friends about the very special magic tapping that Nana Flo had taught her and how it made her feel better.

Even though they thought it seemed a bit weird, Ava and Isaac trusted their friend and agreed to give it a go.

They told Tootsie they were feeling worried. Ava gave her worry a score of nine, and said she could feel it in her head. Isaac scored his a seven, and he could feel it in his tummy.

They began by tapping on their karate chop points three times, just how Nana Flo taught Tootsie.

Then they tapped on the top of their heads, then on the start of their eyebrows, followed by the side of their eyes, under their eyes, under their noses, under their mouths, under their collarbones and finally below their armpits, just like monkeys. They talked about their feelings of being worried as they tapped.

'You know what, I feel a bit better now,' said Ava. 'I've been practising my flying so I'm sure I'll do better than last time.'

'Me too,' said Isaac, 'I'm just going to get in there and do my best for my flying test. That's great magic Tootsie. Thanks!'

Later in the day, Tootsie did her new magic tapping with two of her other friends, Zoe and Rafferty. They were really scared about their upcoming magic spell test because they'd been finding magic spells really tricky to learn.

One day during lessons, Zoe had accidentally turned her teacher into a frog.

And, Rafferty had accidently turned his classmates' hair pink!

It took a long time before their teacher, grumpy Mr Flip, could get everything back to normal, and he wasn't happy! In fact, he was extremely grumpy.

So, once again, Tootsie explained to her friends how Nana Flo's special magic tapping had helped her, and that it also helped Ava and Isaac earlier that day. Zoe and Rafferty thought it sounded pretty cool and agreed to give it a go too.

They told Tootsie where in their bodies they felt their scared feelings, and they both gave their feelings a score out of ten. They talked about their feelings as they tapped. They began tapping on their karate chop points three times, then on the top of their heads, followed by the start of their eyebrows.

Next was the side of their eyes, then under their eyes, under their noses, on the crease on their chins, under their collarbones, and lastly below their armpits, just like monkeys.

Zoe did two rounds of magic tapping and got her score down to zero.

Rafferty did three rounds and got his score down to one. They felt much better, and were no longer feeling scared. In fact both of them were ready to give their magic spell test a go. They agreed that Tootsie's magic tapping was pretty special.

To the surprise and delight of their teachers, including Mr Flip, the young fairies all did so much better in their tests than last term. 'What changed?' their teachers all asked.

'It was Tootsie,' they replied together.

'She taught us a special type of magic that helped us to stop worrying and being scared, so that we could do our very best,' explained Ava.

'Well, you certainly did that. Ava and Isaac, I've never seen you fly so well before,' said a delighted Miss Sparkle, their flying teacher.

'And Zoe and Rafferty, I'm so proud of you, and very relieved!!!' said Mr Flip. 'Both of you have done extremely well today.'

Afterwards, the teachers told Mr Wise, the principal, about what had happened. He called for Tootsie to meet him in his office.

Tootsie was terrified. She'd never been called to the principal's office before, and she had no idea why he wanted to speak to her. She thought that maybe she was going to get into trouble, even though she didn't know why.

On her way to the office, Tootsie began to tremble with fear. Then, she thought about the magic tapping that Nana Flo had taught her – maybe it could help her now!

Tootsie didn't have time to stop and tap on all the magic points, but she remembered to use the magic finger tapping that Nana Flo had shown her for just this sort of situation. So, as she made her way to the office, she tapped on her magic finger points, right next to her fingernails. She reached the office door and knocked politely.

'Come in,' boomed Mr Wise's rather loud voice. Tootsie took a deep breath and entered the office feeling a bit braver, but she kept on tapping on her finger points anyway.

'Well young lady,' boomed Mr Wise, 'It seems you've been doing some new type of magic with some of our students. Could you please explain?'

So Tootsie explained, step by step, the magic tapping that Nana Flo had taught her, and what she had shown her friends.

To her surprise and delight, Tootsie had nothing to be terrified about after all! Mr Wise and the teachers wanted Tootsie to teach them how to do magic tapping as well!

They all thought it was wonderful.

Toosie was asked to show the whole school how to do magic tapping at the next assembly.

This made Tootsie feel nervous, but she tapped for her nervous feelings and she felt much more brave.

Now all of the teachers and kids at Tootsie's school know how to tap.

Even Mr Flip is tapping, and he isn't nearly as grumpy any more!

Their school is a happy, magical, tapping place, where learning is fun, it's ok to make mistakes, and everyone is willing to have a go.

By the way ... Tootsie - the Tapping Fairy - got her tap shoes back, and is still enjoying tapping her way through the day.

FOR PARENTS, TEACHERS & CAREGIVERS

Emotional Freedom Technique (EFT), more commonly known as "Tapping" is a fast and simple evidence-based self-help tool that can be easily learnt and used by adults and children alike. This story is designed to help children learn the technique as well as understand how and when it can be used to help them navigate challenging situations.

Encourage your child to tap along with Tootsie and her friends whilst reading this book together. It's great for them to see you Tapping along too! Repetition will enable them to more readily recall the Tapping points.

After reading about how Tootsie and her friends use Tapping to ease their uncomfortable feelings, help your child to brainstorm a list of situations where Tapping could be a benefit in their daily lives. Practicing together can help your child to become comfortable with formulating their own statements during the Tapping sequence. The trick is to keep it simple, encouraging your child to give voice to their feelings. Don't over-complicate the process.

Incorporating Tapping into every day, even just for a few minutes, can bring about amazing results.

Bigger issues or traumas may require extra support from a trained practitioner.

Jo is available for private and group consultations in person or online. She can be reached via Facebook @jobarkereft or via the Tap Happy website *taphappy.com.au*

THANKS

A huge thank you to all of my friends and family who gave me encouragement and assistance along the way.

Special thanks to Rachael and Jen, Gary, Theresa, Louise, Kylie, Annette & Ian for helping me to find the courage, and belief in myself, that I could somehow bring this idea to completion.

And thank you to all of those who are working in the field of Tapping. Without sharing your belief, commitment, and enthusiasm for this technique far and wide, it wouldn't have found me and this book wouldn't have been possible.

ABOUT THE AUTHOR

Jo Barker is a mum, a nana and an Emotional Freedom Technique (otherwise known as Tapping) and Matrix Reimprinting practitioner. She worked as a primary school teacher for over 25 years.

Jo lives on the Mornington Peninsula in Victoria, Australia with her husband Gary. She loves gardening, cooking for her family, yoga, pilates, her early morning walks on the beach, and spending time with her much loved grandchildren. Jo loves using Tapping to help young and old, but her zone of genius is working with children. She does this in private practice as well as in schools alongside her friend and business partner, Theresa.

After experiencing the benefits of Tapping for herself, and after completing a course to become a practitioner in the field, the idea of Tootsie popped into Jo's head. She just knew this story had to be written so that children could learn, in a fun way, the simple technique of Tapping.

www.ingramcontent.com/pod-product-compliance
Lightning Source LLC
Chambersburg PA
CBHW041428010526
44107CB00045B/1537